RAILROADS OF COLORADO

A Guide to Modern and Narrow Gauge Trains

Steve Shoe   GEORGETOWN LOOP RAILROAD

AN AMERICAN TRAVELER SERIES PUBLICATION

P.R. "Bob" Griswold

2008 Printing

ISBN 13: 978-1-55838-088-2
ISBN 10: 1-55838-088-4

American Traveler Press
A Division of Primer Publishers
5738 North Central Avenue
Phoenix, Arizona 85012
www.AmericanTravelerPress.com
1-800-521-9221

Cover photo courtesy Cumbres & Toltec Scenic Railroad

10 9 8 7 6 5

Printed in China, Published in the United States of America

WELCOME

Just mention Colorado to the avid railfan, and you have his interest; add the term "narrow gauge" and you have his undivided attention. Why this special interest in the Centennial State's railroads? One reason is geography— relatively flat plains in the eastern third of the state, the rugged Rocky Mountains in the central and southwest areas. The railroads traverse all these regions—from the valleys to the mountains. This geographical configuration makes Colorado railroading complex and interesting.

No word in history can compare with "gold" to produce an influx of people and the development of commerce. Add "silver" and the influx becomes a stampede, with all aspects of business booming. These magic words brought the railroads to Colorado when the iron horse was the only reliable and economical means of transportation. Not only did the rails come, they ascended to unbelievable places where the precious metals were being extracted from the peaks. For a mining district to have any semblance of prosperity, a railroad was a necessity.

During the first years of the railroad era in Colorado, developers believed the standard gauge railroad was for the plains and narrow gauge was for the mountains. This belief lasted but a few years because of the American railroad system of interchanging freight and rolling stock between different railroads. The savings in construction and operating costs on the narrow gauge lines were usually outweighed by the costs of transferring freight from the cars of one gauge to the other. Many early narrow gauge railroads thus converted to standard gauge, but some held out, despite the cost of freight interchange. This meant that several 1890-era railroads operated simultaneously with more modern carriers. Such contrasts make Colorado railroading unique.

Railroads of Colorado is part of the ***American Traveler Series***. The other ***Colorado Traveler Guidebooks*** are listed on the back cover of this guide.

Related Titles you should know about:

Arizona Traveler Guidebook:
Arizona's Railroads – Exploring the State By Rail

California Traveler Guidebook:
Railroads Of California – Seeing The State By Rail

Grand Canyon Railroad – Illustrated Guidebook

CONTENTS

S. Rasmussen   SANTA FE NEAR TRINIDAD

Joe Priselac   DENVER & SALT LAKE #119

COLORADO RAILROADING

When the pioneer railroad builders began construction west across "The Great American Desert," their challenge was the Indian who resented the iron horse penetrating his hunting grounds. Once the rails reached the foothills of the Rockies, the challenges were at least as formidable. Building across the plains involved basic engineering skills and a minimum cost per mile; but mountain railroad construction demanded the utmost in civil engineering skill and financing, despite the cost cutting advantage of narrow gauge construction.

To complement the early mining boom, agriculture and commerce also prospered and the railroads served them as well as the mines. The railroad's service to the mines was relatively short-lived. One by one the underground treasures played out and many of the railbeds become ghost trails. Just as rails had been laid to the gold and silver mines, so were they laid to the coal mining districts, and the smelters. But like the precious metal mines, many coal mines played out and alternate sources of power were introduced, again leaving empty, eroded rail tracks.

By then, a new industry was growing in Colorado—tourism. Not only were the mountains a source of precious metals, they were an area of unexcelled scenic grandeur. The dry climate of Colorado's eastern slope was nature's sanitarium where the sick came to be healed. A fashionable vacation was to visit one of the many hot springs resorts. Travelers came in Pullmans, parlor cars, and coaches for a view of the magnificent scenery and to catch trout in rushing mountain streams.

Joe Priselac   CALIFORNIA ZEPHYR

Heavyweight passenger trains such as the Mountain Bluebird, Columbine, Scenic Limited, and Exposition Flyer were followed by the City of Denver, Denver Zephyr, Rocky Mountain Rocket, Colorado Eagle, Super Chief, El Capitan and California Zephyr. Many Colorado towns became railroad centers, Denver and Pueblo being the busiest; Colorado Springs, La Junta, Salida, Alamosa, and Grand Junction were also part of the busy railroad scene and the mining centers of Creede, Cripple Creek, Leadville, and Silverton remained part of the rail activity.

Thankfully, many reminders of Colorado's railroad heritage are still with us. Past and present mingle to create a marvelous scene, telling of pioneer railroad builders and present operators who now compete with other means of transportation, unknown when the first rails reached territorial borders on June 19, 1867.

McClure   NEAR CORONA ON THE MOFFAT ROAD

D&RGW Archives   THE CALIFORNIA ZEPHYR

AMTRAK

Colorado's love for the original California Zephyr is justified because the vista dome that made the Zephyr great was conceived in gorgeous Glenwood Canyon. This Zephyr pride also stems from Burlington Zephyr heritage and the speedy Denver Zephyr from Chicago.

A combination of events made the California Zephyr a reality. First was the construction in 1909 of the Western Pacific Railway, the last transcontinental route. Next came the completion of the Moffat Tunnel in 1928 and the construction of the Dotsero Cutoff in 1934. The Golden Gate International Exposition brought about the Exposition Flyer, a through train from Chicago to San Francisco, operating on Burlington, Denver & Rio Grande Western, and Western Pacific track. The success of the Exposition Flyer inspired the California Zephyr. The first of the 66 stainless steel Zephyr cars began operating in March 1948, the three railroads shared the cost. When completed, the six Zephyr trains included: 18 vista dome coaches, 18 sleepers outfitted with ten roomettes and six double bedrooms each, six baggage cars, six dining cars, six vista dome buffet lounges, six 16-section sleepers, and six vista dome lounge observation cars.

Amtrak   AMTRAK'S CALIFORNIA ZEPHYR

The California Zephyr was planned as a scenic cruise train, with less scenic areas scheduled during the night. The Chicago to San Francisco Bay Trip took 50 hours, not intended to compete with the speedy Union Pacific's City of San Francisco, although on some sections of the Zephyr route, the train reached speeds of 90–100 M.P.H. The 570 scenic miles on the Denver & Rio Grande Western included 46 tunnels through the Colorado Rockies, beginning in South Boulder Canyon to the 6.2 mile Moffat Tunnel under the Continental Divide and through the Fraser River, Byers and Gore Canyons. After the Zephyr left Granby, it followed the Colorado River for 238 spectacular miles, through Glenwood Canyon, Grand Junction, and the Canyon Country into Utah. This magnificent train operated for 21 years.

Today, this passenger route is served by the Amtrak Superliner but the spectacular route is the same. Superliner passengers crowd into the lounge car to get a better view of the mountain scenery west of Denver. Few passengers remain seated as they move from one side of the car to the other to record as much of the trip on film as possible. Of course the photography is interrupted numerous times as the train passes through tunnels. The eastbound Superliner also affords sightseeing with an evening arrival in Denver.

S. Rasmussen — SOUTHWEST CHIEF AT TRINIDAD

Amtrak's Southwest Chief leaves La Junta and the Arkansas Valley to speed southwest through sparsely settled southeast Colorado to Trinidad. This distance of 82 miles is scheduled for 77 minutes. At Trinidad the scene changes dramatically as the Chief turns south on the old Santa Fe tracks past scattered mining towns and an occasional scampering deer to ascend Raton Pass to an elevation of 7,588 feet. Not an impressive elevation by Colorado standards, nevertheless, the grade is dramatic, climbing from Trinidad's 6,000 feet in just 15 miles. Although for most of the route the Chief is a speedster, the 23 miles from Trinidad, Colorado, to Raton, New Mexico, is scheduled for one hour and seven minutes affording an opportunity to enjoy the beautiful mountains and the experience of rolling through the 2,787 foot tunnel at the top of the pass. Darkness usually shrouds the eastbound portion of this trip.

S. Rasmussen — SOUTHWEST CHIEF CLIMBS RATON PASS

Santa Fe Railway   LA JUNTA ROUNDHOUSE & TURNTABLE

THE SANTA FE

Since 1876 when it pushed into Pueblo, the Atchison Topeka and Santa Fe was a part of the Colorado railroad network. After completing its 1880s route over Raton Pass and on to Santa Fe, eventually the AT&SF built north from Pueblo to Denver, paralleling the Denver & Rio Grande. These two single track lines were combined in 1918 to form a double track line between the two cities. La Junta, east of Pueblo, became the center of the Santa Fe's Colorado operation, with a tremendous shop and roundhouse facility. In spite of the new Burlington & Northern Santa Fe name the history remains as fascinating as ever. Today's operation is divided into two functions; Amtrak passenger service and BNSF's intermodal freight operation.

S. Rasmussen   SOUTHBOUND AT LARKSPUR

The joint line south of Denver is the best place to see the Burlington Northern Santa Fe freights. The freights most visible are the coal trains from Wyoming as they climb the 2,000 feet elevation between Denver and Palmer Lake. These trains usually have helpers that uncouple at Palmer Lake. The same parade of freights operate northbound, but the coal trains are empty. This spectacular BNSF freight is visible from U.S. Highway 85 south of Denver to Castle Rock where Interstate Highway 25 follows the rails to Larkspur. Here Colorado State Route 15 parallels the tracks to Palmer Lake, an ideal spot to watch the freights moving in both directions.

P.R. Griswold   BN OAKWAY EMD

BURLINGTON ROUTE

The Burlington in Colorado has had several names beginning with Burlington & Missouri River, then Chicago Burlington & Quincy. Later another pioneer railroad, the Colorado & Southern, merged with Burlington Northern which in turn joined Atchison Topeka & Santa Fe to become the Burlington Northern Santa Fe (BNSF).

The Burlington (or the "Q" as it was generally known) was once famous in Colorado for its stainless steel streamliners: the Denver Zephyr, California Zephyr and Texas Zephyr. Amtrak's Zephyr now operates over Burlington tracks east of Denver to Chicago on the same tracks the Denver Zephyr sped across the prairies.

DENVER & RIO GRANDE WESTERN

Colorado Springs Pioneer Museum
WILLIAM JACKSON PALMER
(1836-1909)

General William Jackson Palmer founded the Denver and Rio Grande Railway. Before coming to Colorado he served with the Cavalry during the Civil War and was involved in establishing the rail route across Arizona to California. In 1870 Palmer's plan was to build a narrow gauge railroad from Denver to El Paso, connecting with rails to Mexico City. First he built a line south along the eastern slope of the mountains, from Denver nearly to the New Mexico state line. The slim gauge tracks never reached El Paso, and it took seven years for the railroad to reach the banks of the Rio Grande at Alamosa. Instead the Denver and Rio Grande spread west to Durango, Silverton, Leadville, Gunnison, Aspen and Grand Junction; later on to Salt Lake City and Ogden, Utah. Palmer did not intend to build a mountain railroad but a conflict at Raton Pass with the Santa Fe Railroad changed his direction from south to west. Not only did General Palmer build his three-foot gauge railroad, but in the process he also founded a number of Colorado

Griswold Collection   DENVER & RIO GRANDE #76

towns, among them Colorado Springs, the first destination of his Denver and Rio Grande Railway.

The network of narrow gauge trackage ultimately reached 1,700 miles, the longest narrow gauge route being Denver to Ogden, Utah, 772 miles. But if the narrow gauge Denver & Rio Grande were to be part of the nationwide

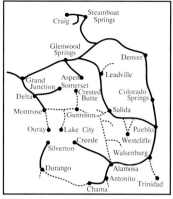

Colorado lines of The Denver and Rio Grande Western.

railroad system, it had to convert to standard gauge. By 1890 the main line to Utah through Royal Gorge, over Tennessee Pass, into Glenwood Canyon, and over Soldier Summit was converted to standard gauge. Some of the mountain narrow gauge lines, especially in southwestern Colorado, served the railroad another 70 plus years and some are still in use by scenic railway successors.

The 20th century brought about the construction of Moffat Tunnel, and the Dotsero Cutoff shortening the route from Denver to Salt Lake City by 173 miles. In 1947 the Denver and Salt Lake was absorbed, putting Steamboat Springs and Craig on the Denver & Rio Grande map. After a short period of Southern Pacific operation, the Denver & Rio Grande Western was absorbed by the Union Pacific Railroad. Now the railroad that went through the mountains became part of the Union Pacific Railroad.

P. R. Griswold   SHAY #14 AT SILVER PLUME

P.R. Griswold   INTERIOR OF COACH

THE DURANGO & SILVERTON NARROW GAUGE RAILROAD

Today travelers ride the same route along the Animas River Canyon between Durango and Silverton that the Denver and Rio Grande Railway completed in 1882. Then the line served Silverton's booming mining district; soon, new narrow gauge sleepers and parlor cars were added to the consists. Before the mines began to play out, three more railroads operated out of Silverton making it a narrow gauge railroad center. Durango was the "Narrow Gauge Capital of the World" for many years, as slim gauge tracks left town in all four directions. When gold and silver production decreased in the San Juan area, railroad service to Silverton lapsed to a sporadic once or twice a week from Durango.

By the 1960s, travelers were heading for Durango specifically to take the scenic 45-mile railroad trip to Silverton. The leisurely, romantic ride took them past ghostly sidings at Hermosa, Rockwood and Needleton, en route to Silverton. Despite efforts by the Denver and Rio Grande Western to discontinue the Silverton train, the passengers kept coming–100,000 a season. Consequently, the Colorado Public Utilities Commission required continued operation. In 1981, Charles E. Bradshaw, Jr. bought the Durango-Silverton line from the Denver & Rio Grande Western. He was determined to make

DURANGO & SILVERTON NARROW GAUGE RR

his Durango and Silverton Narrow Gauge profitable as well as to continue the railroad's historic steam operation. This required tremendous reconditioning and upgrading of equipment and facilities. Bradshaw scoured the country for 1880-era cars, which he painstakingly restored, replacing the oil lamps with electric lighting. Six coal burning locomotives were put into first class operating condition.

At peak season four trains operate, each equipped with restored orange and black coaches and a few open-air roofed gondola cars. The former parlor-buffet car, the Alamosa (from the "San Juan" that operated between Alamosa and Durango until 1951), was rebuilt into a lounge car and is operated daily as an extra fare service. The private cars Nomad and Cinco Animas are available for charter. The Durango and Silverton offers several services such as cars equipped with lifts for the handicapped. The nine-hour round trip includes a layover at Silverton.

Unexcelled scenery is the railroad's main attraction, for the railroad route is not accessible by road. There are also many points of historic interest at both ends of the line: at Durango, the 1882 depot and the Durango & Silverton Narrow Gauge Railroad Museum located in the roundhouse; in Silverton, the entire town is a tour through Colorado's mining history. The Durango and Silverton runs from early May until late October.

CUMBRES & TOLTEC SCENIC RAILROAD

CUMBRES & TOLTEC SCENIC RAILROAD

This narrow gauge steam railroad is the 64-mile remnant of the Denver and Rio Grande Railway's 1880s route between Alamosa and Durango. When prospectors rushed to the fabulously rich San Juan mining area, the Denver & Rio Grande struggled to lay a twisting and turning track to the summit of 10,015 foot Cumbres Pass and across the Continental Divide to reach Durango, a town founded by the railroad. Besides hauling freight to the mines and ores to the smelters, the railroad carried passengers in its new Pullmans and parlor cars.

There was no more delightful trip than the ride between Alamosa and Durango on the luxury "San Juan," complete with parlor car and dining service. Eventually the mines died and passengers and freight switched to highway travel. Denver & Rio Grande service ended in 1967.

But there were those who saw the railroad as a scenic attraction, and persuaded the states of Colorado and New Mexico to purchase the 64 miles of narrow gauge railroad from Antonito, Colorado, to Chama, New Mexico, for $547,120 as a tourist railroad. The states contracted with Kyle Railways, Inc. to operate the Cumbres and Toltec Railroad. Over the years facilities have been upgraded thanks in part to Friends of the Cumbres and Toltec Scenic Railroad, a group of dedicated railfans.

Today trips originate either at Antonito or Chama. Most passengers make the one-day round trip to Osier where lunch is served, and return to their point of origin. The trip from Antonito features a magnificent view of the Sangre de Cristo Range south from Mount Blanca, Mud Tunnel, Rock Tunnel, Garfield Monument and Toltec Gorge; while the trip from Chama provides the opportunity to see the extensive railroad yard, the large collection of narrow gauge rolling stock and the spectacular climb up to Cumbres Pass. Some passengers prefer to take the entire one-way trip between Antonito and Chama and return to their starting point by van on the highway or by rail the following day. The Cumbres and Toltec steam train operates from mid-May to mid-October. The spectacular rugged mountain scenery is sometimes enhanced in the fall by the aspen in glorious golden colors or by an early fall snowstorm.

Rocky Mt. RR Club collection   DENVER, SOUTH PARK & PACIFIC

DENVER SOUTH PARK & PACIFIC

Railfans have a real affection for the Denver South Park and Pacific. This 339-mile narrow gauge line, long since defunct, has its own 11,000-foot-tomb near Pitkin, Alpine Tunnel. Inside the tunnel the rails, ties, and timbers of the South Park remain sealed in an aura of mystery. In 1873 Colorado Governor John Evans incorporated the South Park to run to the new town of Del Norte, in the heart of the San Juan mining area, and (ambitiously) to the Pacific Coast. As the rails were being laid up Platte Canyon, silver was discovered at Leadville, and the race was on. Both the Rio Grande and the South Park reached Buena Vista in 1880. Thanks to negotiations by Jay Gould, for a time both railroads operated to Leadville on a single track. The South Park eventually became part of the Colorado and Southern system, putting it into the same family as the old Colorado Central. Consequently, much of the same equipment that rolled up Platte Canyon also strained up and around the Clear Creek Canyon tracks.

The segment from Leadville to the dormant Climax molybdenum mine is still intact, but in standard gauge form. During the summer months you can ride this section on the Leadville, Colorado & Southern Railroad's diesel powered train. As the train heads toward Fremont Pass, passengers look down on the headwaters of the Arkansas River and Colorado Highway 91. Before returning to Leadville, there are spectacular views of Colorado's highest peak, Mount Elbert. The summer operation extends into early fall with just weekend trips when the aspen trees are in their glorious shades. After these beautiful leaves have fallen, the railroad closes for the winter. Built in 1884, the South Park Depot in Leadville remains the departure point for the Leadville, Colorado & Southern.

S. Rasmussen   LEADVILLE, COLORADO & SOUTHERN

WILLIAM A. H. LOVELAND

Denver Public Library
W. A. H. LOVELAND (1826-1894)

Colorado's first mountain railroad pioneer, William A. H. Loveland, came to Colorado during the 1859 Pikes Peak gold rush. He located in Golden, which became the supply point for the gold mines in the Central City-Blackhawk district. Loveland established the Colorado Central Railroad whose first track went east from Golden to connect with the Denver Pacific, the railroad from Cheyenne to Denver. His Colorado Central developed into a railroad of different gauges, narrow in the mountains and standard on the plains. In 1872 the Colorado Central standard gauge was surveyed from near Golden to Julesburg at the Nebraska border, but it was not built for several years. In 1877 his plans were changed to a route meeting the Union Pacific west of Cheyenne which would give the UP a route into Golden and Denver. Later the Union Pacific acquired the Denver Pacific and the tracks from Julesburg were completed in 1881. Loveland's Colorado Central thus became part of the Union Pacific.

The better-known segment of the Colorado Central was the narrow gauge Clear Creek Division serving the rich mining areas. Even this short distance of railroad was difficult for Loveland to complete, and it was not until the end of 1872 that the Colorado Central reached Blackhawk. The next completion was to Georgetown in 1877, followed by the steep extension to Central City in 1878. Loveland had ideas of crossing the Continental Divide near Loveland Pass, but before he could make a survey, the Union Pacific had leased his railroad. The most famous segment of the Colorado Central, the Georgetown Loop between Georgetown and Silver Plume, was therefore built after the railroad passed from Loveland's control.

J.C. Thode collection   GEORGETOWN LOOP

THE GEORGETOWN LOOP

The Union Pacific Railroad organized the Georgetown Leadville and San Juan Railway with the plan to build west from Georgetown primarily to reach Leadville. Captain E.L. Berthoud began the survey in 1879, but was soon replaced by Jacob Blickensderfer. The plans lay dormant until 1882 when construction began west from Georgetown to Silver Plume just two miles distant, but 638 feet higher. To reach Silver Plume, 4-½ miles of track had to be laid to accomplish the steep climb, a grade of nearly three percent. The track headed west up the Clear Creek Valley then reversed direction, always climbing, and crossed over the lower track on a 300-foot trestle 75 feet above the first track. The track continued twisting and re-crossing Clear Creek until it reached Silver Plume.

Upon completion in 1884, the high bridge in a canyon of superb mountain scenery became an instant tourist attraction. For 40 years, travelers flocked to view this spectacular engineering achievement. The railroad never reached Leadville; in fact, it was built only a few miles beyond Silver Plume to Graymont. But the Argentine Central Railway carried travelers from Silver Plume to the mining town of Waldorf and on to the summit of Mount McClellan— more than 14,000 feet in elevation. Also the Sunshine Peak Aerial Railway (a tram) took the more daring tourists in oversized mine buckets up the side of the mountain from Silver Plume to a 13,000-foot elevation.

As the mines played out and autos gained popularity, the narrow gauge "Loop" was no longer needed. In 1927, all passenger trains on the Clear Creek Lines were discontinued.

Dwayne Easterling   RECONSTRUCTED GEORGETOWN LOOP

A few freight trains went to Silver Plume until 1938, but the following year the rails were removed and the spectacular loop bridge torn down and sold for scrap.

In the 1960s, the Colorado Historical Society initiated a restoration plan to include a living history museum near the Lebanon Mine between Georgetown and Silver Plume. The idea included rebuilding at least a section of the narrow gauge railroad. Gradually support grew for actually rebuilding the railroad between Georgetown and Silver Plume. The Silver Plume depot was salvaged and the Colorado Highway Department cooperated in the Interstate Highway 70 construction so that the railroad grade would not be disturbed. In the 1970s, the Seabees began rebuilding the narrow gauge tracks east from Silver Plume to the south approach of the high "Devil's Gate Viaduct." The Colorado Historical Society arranged for the operation of the new Georgetown Loop Railroad, and the Denver & Rio Grande Western furnished some freight cars from the remains of its terminated narrow gauge operation at Alamosa. Sufficient rolling stock was moved from the tourist railroad at Central City to carry passengers over the new section of track from Silver Plume.

In 1982, the Boettcher Foundation made a grant of $1,000,000 to rebuild the "High Bridge" at Devil's Gate, assuring completion of the Georgetown Loop. With the help of additional grants the "High Bridge" reconstruction was completed in 1986. Rebuilding the railroad continued with the construction of the engine house in Silver Plume. The railroad operates its ticket office, gift shop and restaurant in the original brick Georgetown Depot.

P.R. Griswold   GEORGETOWN LOOP

The Georgetown Loop Railroad owns three Shay locomotives from logging railroads and two conventional piston locomotives from the International Railways of Central America. All these steam locomotives are oil burners. Like most railroads, diesels have invaded the system. They are used for switching at Silver Plume and occasional passenger trips. A Georgetown Loop acquisition is the classic 1902 coach "Tahoe" from the Lake Tahoe Railway & Transportation Company in California. This beautifully restored car is occasionally used on the run to Silver Plume.

From Memorial day through September the line carries passengers over the "Far Famed Georgetown Loop" on a round trip that includes an optional educational tour of the Lebanon Mine.

THE COLORADO MIDLAND

Denver Public Library
JAMES JOHN HAGERMAN

Tuberculosis brought millionaire James J. Hagerman to Colorado Springs in October 1884. The salubrious Colorado climate transformed Hagerman into a businessman vitally interested in the newly planned Colorado Midland Railway from Colorado Springs to Leadville and Aspen. In 1886 when the Colorado Midland began building west through Ute Pass, Aspen's silver potential was highly speculative. But when Aspen's mines began producing, the race was on between the Denver & Rio Grande's narrow gauge and Hagerman's new standard gauge Colorado Midland. The Denver & Rio

Grande won the race, but by early 1888 the Colorado Midland was also operating to Aspen, sharing the booming business.

The Colorado Midland proved that standard gauge trains could operate in the Colorado mountains. This forced the Denver & Rio Grande to standard gauge its line through Glenwood Canyon to Grand Junction and Salt Lake City. The Colorado Midland continued to Glenwood Springs and New Castle, then by way of the Rio Grande Junction Railroad to Grand Junction. But this new standard gauge line was greatly disadvantaged by the Hagerman Tunnel which crossed the Continental Divide at 11,528 feet. To combat winter snows a lower altitude tunnel, the Busk-Ivanhoe, was bored through the Divide 500 feet lower. The improvement still failed to make the operation practical in spite of the use of rotary snowplows.

CO Hist. Society   ROTARY SNOWPLOW ON THE COLORADO MIDLAND

During World War I the Railroad Administration diverted all through traffic from the Colorado Midland to the Denver & Rio Grande, so that by 1921 the railroad was gone except for 29 miles from Colorado Springs to Divide which was purchased by Midland Terminal to operate its ore trains from Cripple Creek. That remaining segment lasted until 1949. J.J. Hagerman was also involved in the wealthy Molly Gibson mine at Aspen, coal mines at New Castle, gold mines at Cripple Creek, banking, and agriculture.

P.R. Griswold   CRIPPLE CREEK & VICTOR

THE CRIPPLE CREEK & VICTOR RAILROAD

The Cripple Creek and Victor is a little railroad, about two miles long with a gauge of only two feet. Its home is the site of Colorado's last and biggest gold strike, when the area was served by three railroads and two interurban lines. The railroad's tracks are on the grade of the Midland Terminal Railroad, the last railroad to serve this mining area through its decline until the last train operated in 1949. The Cripple Creek & Victor operates its two-foot gauge over the standard gauge grade of the Midland Terminal. The line begins in Cripple Creek near the old three-story Midland Terminal depot, now a museum. The Cripple Creek and Victor has its own depot near the site of the Midland Terminal engine house. Its depot is an antique itself as it once served as the depot at Bull Hill.

The Cripple Creek & Victor has an impressive stable of iron horses. Its workhorse is the Vista Grande, a 1927 diamond stack Porter. Purchased in Mexico, it sports a brass star on the front of the boiler. The Goldfield is an 0-4-4-0 Mallet built by Orenstein-Koppel in Germany in 1902. This black locomotive #1 with red and silver trim has a straight stack, a vintage headlight, and a distinctive shrill European whistle. The Montezuma, an 0-4-0 Henshel with a straight stack, has a square headlight and a most unusual wooden cab. The railroad also owns an 0-4-4-0 Bagnal Ltd. 26-ton engine built in Stafford, England which came to Cripple Creek from Sezela, Natal, Africa. The elevation at Cripple Creek is 9,522 feet so bring a sweater for the spectacular journey to the Mary McKinney Mine.

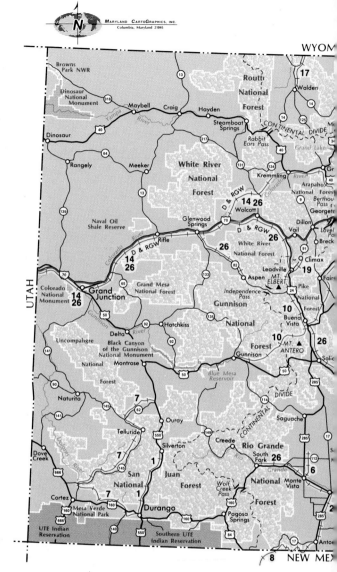

MARYLAND CARTOGRAPHICS, INC.
Columbia, Maryland 21045

WYOM

Browns Park NWR

Dinosaur National Monument

13

Routt National Forest

17

Walden

318

Maybell

Craig

Hayden

Steamboat Springs

14

125

Me

CONTINENTAL DIVIDE

Dinosaur

40

Yampa River

Rabbit Ears Pass

Grand Lake

40

34

Gr

Rangely

64

Meeker

White River National Forest

317

131

Kremmling

Colorado River

40

139

13

Arapaho National Forest

9

Berthou Pass

Georgetc

D & RGW

14 26

Wolcott

Naval Oil Shale Reserve

Glenwood Springs

70

Dillon

Loveli Pa

Breck

D & RGW

Vail

91

Rifle

Colorado River

D & RGW

26

White River National Forest

26

Climax

14 26

82

Leadville

MT. ELBERT ▲

19

Faire

Colorado National Monument

70

65

Grand Mesa National Forest

133

Aspen

Independence Pass

Pike National

24

10

Grand Junction

14 26

Gunnison National

135

Buena Vista

50

Gunnison River

92

Hotchkiss

10

MT. ANTERO ▲

26

Delta

92

Salic

Uncompahgre

Black Canyon of the Gunnison National Monument

141

Montrose

Forest

50

Blue Mesa Reservoir

285

National

Forest

90

Naturita

7

62

DIVIDE

116

Saguache

141

149

Ouray

CONTINENTAL

285

17

Telluride

550

Creede

Rio Grande

Dove Creek

Dolores River

7

145

Silverton

1

San Juan National Forest

149

South Fork

26

6

666

Cortez

7

145

1

Wolf Creek Pass

National

Monte Vista

Mesa Verde National Park

160

160

Durango

160

Forest

2

160

UTE Indian Reservation

666

Pagosa Springs

285

140

550

Southern UTE Indian Reservation

84

17

Anto

8

NEW MEX

---

0 10 20 30 40 50 Miles

0 10 20 30 40 50 Kilometers

For a larger scale map of Colorado railroads, both operating and abandoned, consult the Colorado Railroad Museum's Colorado Railroad Map.

4   Atchison Topeka & Santa Fe tracks (BI

11 Burlington Northern Railway tracks (B

21 Colorado Railroad Museum

15 Coors Railroad

9   Cripple Creek & Victor Narrow Gauge

8   Cumbres & Toltec Scenic Railroad

14 Denver & Rio Grande Western (D&RC

1   Durango & Silverton Narrow Gauge R

20 Forney Transportation Museum

23 Georgetown Loop Railroad

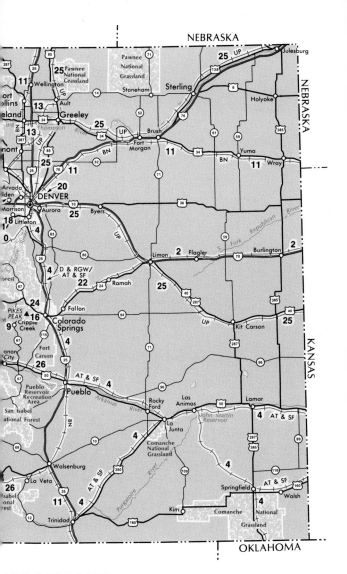

ADO RAILROADS

J.C. Newell   DENVER UNION STATION

THE GRAND DEPOTS

Denver's Union Station opened in 1881 as a joint venture of the Denver and Rio Grande, Union Pacific, and Colorado Central. Amtrak's Superliner Zephyr and, on winter weekends, the Rio Grande Ski Train still receive and deliver passengers at Denver's Union Station. The station has been rebuilt and renovated several times. The present center section, track sheds and subways to the tracks were added in 1914 and 1915. From 1906 to 1931, the 70-ton Welcome Arch at the foot of 17th Street lighted the entrance to Union Station with 1,600 bulbs. Over the years, Union Station housed such affiliated businesses as express companies and the Post Office Terminal Annex. Both narrow and standard gauge and the resulting three rail tracks served the station. The electrical overhead for the Denver and Interurban was on one side of the building and on the other were the 3'6" tracks of the Denver Tramway Loop. In the basement, the Denver Society of Model Engineers display their "O" gauge model layout dating back to 1935.

Pueblo's Union Depot was built in 1889. The three-story Victorian structure once served passengers of the Denver & Rio Grande Western, Colorado & Southern, Atchison Topeka & Santa Fe, Missouri Pacific, and Chicago Rock Island & Pacific. On its upper floors were hotel facilities and offices for railroad personnel. On the ground floor a ticket counter, spacious waiting room and dining room. Today the upper floors are apartments and the station area is now a commercial complex. The imposing clock tower has been preserved. Outside on the unused station tracks is a unique collection of rolling stock.

courtesy Pueblo Union Depot

P. R. Griswold Collection   BLANCA'S "GRAND" UNION STATION

P.R. Griswold   LOADING IN THE PARK

THE FORT COLLINS TROLLEY

The Fort Collins Trolley began operation in Denver December 29, 1907, with 44-passenger cars from the Woeber Car Works also of Denver. The system was operated by the Denver and Interurban Railroad, a subsidiary of the Colorado and Southern Railroad. By 1914 two lines connected to form a loop, making the entire system about seven miles long. Six cars and two trailers handled the business until the automobile came along and severely reduced patronage to the point where operation was suspended.

The City of Fort Collins bought the defunct system for $75,000 and purchased four A.C.F. Birney cars (#20-23). By 1924 it had added three more Birneys (#24-26) in a continuous effort to maintain a better streetcar system than its rival city, Greeley. Fort Collins continued a good five-cent fare streetcar system until its cars just plain wore out; the last operating on June 30, 1951. Car #22 went to the Rocky Mountain Railroad Club and is now at the Colorado Railroad Museum, #21 went to the Pioneer Museum. Later Car #21 was restored by the Fort Collins Municipal Railway Society and usually runs between downtown and the city park on weekends and holidays.

P.R. Griswold   IN THE LOVELAND YARD

GREAT WESTERN RAILWAY

This railroad began operating to serve the four beet sugar factories of Great Western Sugar at Loveland, Longmont, Windsor, and Eaton. Later it would serve the company's molasses treatment and monosodium glutamate plants at Johnstown. The Great Western grew to a 155-mile railroad responsible for hauling freight for the beet factories. In the major beet months from October to January, the line handled as many as 10,000 cars of beets. In pre-automobile days, Great Western also provided passenger service, handling about 10,000 passengers annually. After 1926, passengers rode in combination coach #100 (now at the Colorado Railroad Museum) in mixed trains; eventually this open platform car was replaced by a caboose.

Great Western was best known for three steam engines, #51, #75, and #90 which operated long after the steam era. The last one, #90, left the railroad in 1967. Great Western Sugar declared bankruptcy in 1985, signaling the end of sugar beet processing, but the railroad managed to survive. Headquartered in Loveland, this freight-only short line railroad is often spotted in Fort Collins and Greeley.

J.R. Jones   CROSSING INTERSTATE 25

Griswold Collection   MANITOU & PIKES PEAK

MANITOU & PIKES PEAK COG RAILWAY

The fame of Pikes Peak, perhaps America's most famous mountain, dates back to the days of the Santa Fe Trail. The view from the peak inspired Katherine Lee Bates to write *America the Beautiful* and celebrates the incomparable view from the summit. Zalmon G. Simmons of mattress fame is credited with promoting the idea of a railroad to the summit after making the trip on a mule. From the time the Manitou and Pikes Peak Railway was organized in 1888, it was three years before regular trains operated to the summit. Every spring since then the snow drifts are plowed out so visitors can ride the Manitou & Pikes Peak Railway.

For more than 60 years 16% tilted flat-nosed steam engines that looked like the front end had been involved in some kind of mishap pushed the single car tourist trains to

D.T. Arndt   THE COG ROAD IN MAY

the barren summit for an unsurpassed view. In those early days, travelers detrained in Colorado Springs at the Denver & Rio Grande or Santa Fe depots, six or seven miles from the Cog Road depot. Another D&RG train or the Colorado Springs and Interurban streetcar took the traveler to Manitou, where they boarded the Manitou Electric Railway and Casino Company streetcar up the hill to the Cog Road depot.

Today the trip is more convenient but just as spectacular in sleek new Swiss-built diesel cars. Past the stately spruces and the jagged rocks of Englemann Canyon, the train begins its ascent of the six percent grade. The grade increases and the panorama turns more awesome as the train passes Minnehaha, Son of a Gun Hill, Halfway House (not halfway), and Ruxton Park. The higher it climbs, the greater the view. Railfans can also marvel at the engineering of a railroad that takes them up almost 8,000 feet in just 8.9 miles.

P.R. Griswold   COG ROAD LOCOMOTIVE

THE MOFFAT TUNNEL

Denver Public Library
DAVID H. MOFFAT (1839-1911)

Long before David Moffat received his acclaim as a railroad builder, he was one of Colorado's wealthiest men and greatest public benefactors. He came to Denver in 1860 as a banker, and in association with Jerome B. Chaffee, ultimately purchased nearly a hundred mines, some of them producers of fabulous wealth. Moffat was involved in railroad building from the time the Denver Pacific reached Denver from Cheyenne in 1870. When silver was discovered at Leadville, he was active in the syndicate that built the Denver South Park and Pacific. His other railroad projects included the Boulder Valley, the Golden Boulder and Caribou, the Rio Grande Gunnison, and the Florence and Cripple Creek. While Moffat was president of the then narrow gauge Denver & Rio Grande his line competed with the standard gauge Colorado Midland to reach the mines at Aspen. When the enormously wealthy silver mines at Creede were discovered, Moffat planned to build nine miles of railroad from Wagon Wheel Gap to Creede, but his New York board of directors disagreed. Undaunted, he resigned and built the railroad to Creede on his own.

When the Union Pacific crossed the Continental Divide through Wyoming in 1868, many Colorado men, Moffat among them, envisioned a railroad from Denver to the Pacific Coast. While president of the Denver & Rio Grande, he had surveys made for such a route, but New

Clifford Betts Collection   FIRST TRAIN THRU TUNNEL 2/26/28

York directors rebuffed his efforts. Moffat persisted in his dream and in 1902 organized the Denver Northwestern and Pacific Railway for a line west to Salt Lake. His plan was to tunnel under the Continental Divide near Rollins Pass, then to serve coal rich areas of northwestern Colorado on the way west. This time the competing transcontinental railroads under Harriman and Gould successfully shut off the money supply, thwarting Moffat's threat of a new direct route west. Instead of going through the mountain, he was forced to go over it at an elevation of 11,600 feet. Moffat spent his own fortune, some $10 million, but he lived only to see his railroad reach Steamboat Springs. After his death in 1911 the rails inched on to Craig, but never reached Utah. Seventeen years later, the tunnel was completed under the Continental Divide.

The monument to David Moffat, the 6.2-mile Moffat Tunnel, was begun in the fall and winter of 1923-24 and was actually two tunnels. The 8 x 8-foot pioneer bore, 75 feet from the main tunnel, would ultimately serve as a water diversion tunnel. At an elevation slightly over 9,000 feet, the 16 x 24-foot railroad tunnel eliminated the winter conditions that trains encountered 2,000 feet higher on Rollins Pass. On February 26, 1928, the first train emerged from the tunnel, culminating four years of hazardous underground construction that claimed the lives of 19 workmen.

The route known as Moffat Road has operated under many names: Denver, Northwestern & Pacific Railway; Denver & Salt Lake Railway; Denver & Rio Grande Western Railroad; Southern Pacific Lines; and Union Pacific. Today's travelers can traverse the Moffat Tunnel on Amtrak or the seasonal Rio Grande Ski Train.

P.R. Griswold   WEST PORTAL MOFFAT TUNNEL

Matt Anderson   RIO GRANDE SKI TRAIN

RIO GRANDE SKI TRAIN

As early as 1913 the Denver Northwestern and Pacific (Moffat Road) operated a "Snow Train" over Corona Pass to Hot Sulphur Springs. Then in 1928 came the Moffat Tunnel and West Portal station was the destination for skiers. Ultimately West Portal evolved into the Winter Park Ski Area. The first ski trains to Winter Park operated on the Denver and Salt Lake. The Denver & Rio Grande Ski Train began operation in 1947.

The 14-car Rio Grande Ski Train includes two café lounge cars. The train has a capacity of 750 making it the largest scheduled passenger train in the country. Pulled by Amtrak engines the train climbs the 2% grade through South Boulder Canyon with its 28 tunnels and the 6.2 mile Moffat Tunnel before reaching Winter Park. Probably half the passengers on the Ski Train are not skiers but sightseers. Depending on snow conditions the season is usually from mid-December to mid-April.

D.T. Arndt   RIO GRANDE SKI TRAIN

RIO GRANDE SOUTHERN RAILWAY

Denver Public Library
OTTO MEARS (1840-1931)

The Pathfinder of the San Juan, Otto Mears, had been a prominent Coloradan for 20 years before he began railroad building. He was a merchant, Indian agent, politician, and builder of toll roads to nearly inaccessible places, including Leadville. As mining camps developed in the San Juan Mountains, Mears built a network of toll roads in southwestern Colorado to connect the remote towns with the outside world. Once Mears had toll roads throughout the San Juans, he thought it logical to take up railroad building. Starting in 1888, he built north from Silverton along Mineral Creek to Red Mountain Pass as far as Albany where the stagecoach continued over Mears' toll road to Ouray. Frustrated by the seemingly impossible rail route into Ouray from the south, he organized the Rio Grande Southern Railroad and made an end run from Durango to Ridgway ten miles north of Ouray.

The Rio Grande Southern began as Otto Mear's 162-mile detour from Durango to Ridgway. Enroute the railroad served the mines of Telluride, Ophir, and Rico; it was completed in 1891, just two years before the silver collapse of 1893. Otto Mears lost the Rio Grande Southern, but the railroad survived under control of the Denver and Rio Grande. The mountain narrow gauge hauled coal from Hesperus and Porter to the smelter at Durango. Livestock and lumber shipments also kept the freight trains rolling.

An "Around the Circle" trip on the Denver and Rio Grande and Rio Grande Southern was popular with summer tourists. The trip from Denver went though the Royal Gorge, over Marshall Pass and through the Black Canyon of the Gunnison before reaching the Rio Grande Southern at Ridgeway. The Rio Grande Southern portion of the trip went to Telluride then through Lizard Head Pass to Dolores and a visit to Mesa Verde National Park. From there the circle continued through Durango, back onto the Denver & Rio Grande track to Chama, Alamosa, and return to Denver. A thousand miles through deep canyons and over high trestles all for the fare of $28.00.

Griswold collection   THE GALLOPING GOOSE

When a nationwide depression hit in the 1930s, the Rio Grande Southern was able to continue service with its new invention, the Galloping Goose. This strange bird was a combination second-hand Buick or Pierce Arrow automobile with a Wayne bus body mounted on flanged wheels and a compartment attached behind for less than carload freight. The passengers rode in the automobile. The Galloping Goose with an economical one man operation gave the "Southern" twenty extra years of life. The end came in 1951.

Rocky Mountain Railroad Club
RIO GRANDE SOUTHERN #20 NEAR VANCE JUNCTION

SAN LUIS CENTRAL 1950

THE SAN LUIS CENTRAL

The San Luis Central locally dubbed the "Pea Vine" is a 12-mile agricultural railroad between Monte Vista and Center. Originated in 1913, it was built to serve the San Luis Valley's beet sugar factory. Only one year after the railroad was built, the factory closed, but the standard gauge railroad continued hauling out agricultural products and bringing back merchandise. The railroad's only steam engine, "Little Nell," handled all the trains–up to 114 cars– for more than 40 years before it was replaced by a 600 horsepower diesel in 1955.

Today the "Pea Vine" often has more area business than the larger Denver & Rio Grande Western to which it connects at Sugar Junction, just east of Monte Vista. The San Luis Central has been a successful shortline since its inception.

.R. Griswold

AT SUGAR JUNCTION

S. Rasmussen HERE COMES THE SANTA FE!

THE ROYAL GORGE WAR

For seven years the Santa Fe had been building west from Topeka, Kansas along the old Santa Fe Trail, attempting to replace the slow moving wagons heading to Santa Fe with trade goods. Two railroads had planned to construct lines through Raton Pass just south of Trinidad; the Santa Fe on standard gauge, the Denver & Rio Grande on narrow gauge. The Santa Fe crew beat the Rio Grande men to the pass by just a few hours which seemed to assure them the better route. Until this 1878 meeting, General Palmer of the Rio Grande had not considered the Santa Fe a competitor neither had he considered young William B. Strong a formidable adversary. Obviously he was wrong–Strong not only planned to build to Santa Fe and on to the Pacific Coast but to Leadville. His plans to go south thwarted, Palmer decided to take his well-suited narrow gauge into the mountains to reach the silver mines. Thus, both railroads found themselves headed to Leadville through the 30-foot wide Royal Gorge of the Arkansas River, a chasm barely wide enough for one railroad. Simultaneously the railroads moved construction crews to the Royal Gorge and hired thugs to protect the workers from their rivals. The Santa Fe supposedly imported Bat Masterson from Dodge City to lead its militant forces. While two armed groups were

ROYAL GORGE RAILROAD

indeed at the Royal Gorge, and while some fortifications were built, telegraph wires cut, and messages sent in code, the physical fighting was minimal. Most of the battling was done in the courts.

The court found in favor of the Rio Grande but not without cost. Jay Gould now entered the Rio Grande family and arranged a fair settlement via the "Treaty of Boston," which for 10 years prohibited the Rio Grande from building farther south than Espanola, New Mexico. The pact prohibited the Santa Fe from building west of the Rio Grande tracks in Colorado. The Rio Grande was ordered to pay the Santa Fe $1,400,000 for the grade it had built toward Leadville, but the Denver & Rio Grande now owned the route, changing it from a north-south railroad to an east-west carrier.

DEEP IN THE GRAND CANYON OF THE ARKANSAS

D. Strickler   SANTA FE DEPOT CAÑON CITY

THE ROYAL GORGE ROUTE

In 1998 the then dormant Denver & Rio Grande route through the Royal Gorge was sold by Union Pacific to the Cañon City & Royal Gorge Railroad. The 24 mile route through the Grand Canyon of the Arkansas is now described as "The most arresting scenic site in all of American railroading." The two hour trip crosses over a "Hanging Bridge" suspended from the canyon walls as the diesel train traverses the 1000 foot deep Gorge. Glimpses of red-tailed hawks and big horned sheep along with views of stone ruins from the Royal Gorge War and geologic wonders are all part of the scenery. The Royal Gorge Route departs from the 1914 Santa Fe Depot in Cañon City. The train operates year round on weekends and daily during the summer and early fall.

S. Rasmussen   THE HANGING BRIDGE

Colorado Railroad Museum STEAM-UP

COLORADO RAILROAD MUSEUM

The extensive, privately funded Colorado Railroad Museum, the largest railroad museum in the Rocky Mountain Area contains more than 70 pieces of rare railroad rolling stock, several owned by the Rocky Mountain Railroad Club and the National Railway Historical Society. Most cars and locomotives are narrow gauge, some dating to the 1870s, but pieces of standard gauge rolling stock are also displayed. Their show piece is the Denver & Rio Grande's 1881 narrow gauge locomotive #346, the oldest operating locomotive in Colorado. The museum crew periodically fires up this antique and operates over a few hundred feet of track, pulling two or three vintage passenger cars.

.R. Griswold GALLOPING GOOSE #2

The masonry building, a replica of an 1880s depot, houses railroad artifacts, photographs, and the Richardson Research Library. The gift shop features timetable reprints and railroad books. In the museum basement is the remarkable layout of the Denver HO Model Railroad Club. The location in Golden is in a good railroad neighborhood, just across the street from the busy Burlington Northern Santa Fe track. Also in Golden is the Coors Railroad.

P.R. Griswold   FOUR WHEEL CABOOSE CO RR MUSEUM

COORS RAILROAD

Crowded between North and South Table Mountain in the Clear Creek Valley is the Coors Brewery and its railroad with four separate yards that serve the brewery operation. The Coors Railroad owns five ex-Rock Island SW8 switchers (C-987 through C-991) and one SW1001 C-998. Another interesting piece of motive power is the Whiting Corporation trackmobile used to move a single car when necessary. The rolling stock are the 132 white bulk beer cars used to ship the product to the Coors facility at Elkton, Virginia. These cars, numbered in the CORX 5000 series, have a 20,886-gallon capacity–672 barrels of beer per car.

Although they never leave the Coors yard, the railroad owns eight specially designed covered hopper cars (CORX 1001-1008) to transport grain from the silos near the east end of the yard to the brewery at the opposite end. A red switcher handles this operation.

P.R. Griswold   COORS ENGINE 998 & BULK BEER CARS

The Burlington Northern Santa Fe operates two freights a day from Denver to Golden, mostly 65-car trains going to Coors delivering empty bottles, cans for recycling, and kegs for reuse, plus hopper cars of grain and coal. Parsons ammonia is also delivered by the tank carload for the brewery's spotless maintenance. After delivering cars to the east end of the yard the BNSF moves to Coors North Yard where it picks up loaded box cars for an eastbound train.

Visitors are welcome at the brewery but the railroad yards are off limits. Fortunately, the bridge on McIntyre Street gives an excellent view of the railroad yard.

Rasmussen   BNSF BEER TRAIN AT GOLDEN

Union Pacific Railroad   BIG BOY #8444

THE UNION PACIFIC

In years past, the Union Pacific in Colorado was confined to the northeast quadrant of the state when passenger trains like the Columbine and Portland Rose steamed into Denver. Then came the yellow streamliners headed by the famous City of Denver, but they disappeared when Amtrak took over rail passenger service.

With Southern Pacific becoming part of Union Pacific its freights operate all over the state even into Craig Somerset, Cañon City and Antonito, once strongholds of the Denver & Rio Grande Western. The major portion of their transcontinental freight crosses north through Wyoming but the big yellow Union Pacific diesels can also be spotted on the Moffat Tunnel route.

S. Conners   UNION PACIFIC DIESEL

TRAIN WRECKS

Despite the hazards of mountain railroads, three of Colorado's worst train wrecks occurred near each other on standard gauge lines on the eastern plains. On May 14, 1888, a Santa Fe freight from Pueblo arrived at Colorado Springs at 2:05 a.m. where the crew unloaded three cars, leaving the last five cars of the train on the main line with the brakes set. Midway through the unloading, the crew noticed that the five rear cars were gone—headed back toward Pueblo on a down grade! Headed north from Pueblo was the four-car passenger train #7, which arrived at Fountain at 2:41 a.m. and took water. The crew heard the runaway cars rolling down the track about 40 M.P.H. (good speed for 1888) and sensing disaster, escaped the crash. But among the runaways were a tank car containing 3,000 gallons of naptha, and a car carrying 18 tons of explosive powder. The freight cars crashed into the passenger locomotive, ignited the naptha, and fire erupted all over the area. Fortunately the passenger cars could be rolled back from the blaze, but the explosion that followed was felt as far away as Colorado Springs and Pueblo, resulting in three fatalities and 28 injuries. The blast blew a hole 15 feet deep and 35 feet wide and damaged nearly every building in Fountain.

Courtesy of Pueblo County Hist. Soc.   ORIGINAL PUEBLO UNION DEPOT

Built in 1889. After the 1921 flood, the clock tower was reduced in height for safety reasons.

Eden, just a few miles south of Fountain was the site of a crash resulting in 97 fatalities. On August 7, 1904, a cloudburst in Hogan's Gulch sent a torrent downstream that weakened the D&RG bridge. The D&RG/Missouri Pacific #11 (the Denver, Kansas City, St. Louis Express), a six-car train with 162 passengers and crew, left Colorado Springs at 7:10 p.m. Locomotive #1009 fell just short of making the tottering bridge, plunging into the raging torrent with three other cars. It was days before some of the bodies were found in the wrecked cars that had been washed far downstream into Fountain Creek.

Damage caused by the great flood in Pueblo on June 4, 1921, caused one of Colorado's worst railroad disasters. Two stranded passenger trains, Denver &Rio Grande #3 and Missouri Pacific #14, were caught in the swirling debris rushing down the Arkansas River, resulting in seven deaths. The major railroad yards were all in the path of the flood, the D&RG alone had 468 cars turned over or demolished. For days, all traffic through Pueblo stopped, and it was months before the damage was completely repaired.

J.C. Thode collection   THE PUEBLO FLOOD

AT THE TINY TOWN STATION

EXHIBITS AND DISPLAYS

Located in Morrison, **Tiny Town** is a model railroad that travels through a one-sixth scale village. The mile long track, first laid in 1915 carries two live steam and two diesel locomotives. Riding the train is a delightful experience for children.

FORNEY LOCOMOTIVE AT FORNEY MUSEUM

Forney Museum has an impressive collection of railroad equipment. The museum originated in Fort Collins but is now located in Denver. The Forney locomotive in the collection was built in 1897.

RAIL FINDER

AMTRAK
Denver Union Station
1701 Wynkoop Street
Denver, Colorado 80202
(800) 872-7245
www.amtrak.com

Colorado Railroad Museum
17155 West 44th Avenue
Golden, Colorado 80402
(800) 365-6263
www.crrm.org

**Cañon City & Royal Gorge
  Railroad**
Santa Fe Depot
330 Royal Gorge Boulevard
Cañon City, Colorado 81212
(888) 724-5748
www.RoyalGorgeRoute.com

**Cripple Creek & Victor Narrow
  Gauge Railroad**
5th and Bennett Avenue
Cripple Creek, Colorado 80813
(719) 689-2640
www.CrippleCreekRailroad.com

**Cumbres & Toltec Scenic
  Railroad**
Colorado Depot
5250 US Highway 285
Antonito, Colorado 81120
(888) 286-2737
www.CumbresToltec.com

**Durango & Silverton Narrow
  Gauge Railroad**
479 Main Avenue
Durango, Colorado 81301
(877) 872-4607
www.DurangoTrain.com

Forney Transportation Museum
4303 Brighton Boulevard
Denver, Colorado 80216
(303) 297-1113
www.ForneyMuseum.com

Fort Collins Trolley
Fort Collins Municipal Railway
  Society
1500 West Oak Street
Fort Collins, Colorado 80521
(970) 224-5372
www.fortnet.org/trolley/

Georgetown Loop Railroad
Devil's Gate Station
646 Loop Drive
Georgetown, Colorado 80444
(888) 456-6777
www.GeorgetownLoopRR.com

**Leadville, Colorado & Southern
  Railroad**
326 East 7th Street
Leadville, Colorado 80461
(866) 386-3936
www.Leadville-Train.com

**Manitou & Pikes Peak Cog
  Railway**
515 Ruxton Avenue
Manitou Springs, Colorado 8082▪
(719) 685-5401
www.CogRailway.com

Pueblo Railway Museum
Pueblo Union Depot
132 West B Street
Pueblo, Colorado 81003
(719) 544-1773
www.PuebloRailway.org

Platt Valley Trolley
Denver Rail Heritage Society
2785 North Speer Boulevard
Denver, Colorado 80211
(303) 458-6255
www.DenverTrolley.org

Regional Transportation Distric▪
1600 Blake Street
Denver, Colorado 80202
(800) 366-7433
www.RTD-Denver.com

Rio Grande Scenic Railroad
601 State Street
Alamosa, Colorado 81101
(877) 726-7245
www.AlamosaTrain.com

Rio Grande Ski Train
Denver Union Station
17th & Wynkoop Street
Denver, Colorado 80202
(303) 296-4754
www.SkiTrain.com

Tiny Town Railway
6249 South Turkey Creek Road
Tiny Town, Colorado 80465
(303) 697-6829
www.TinyTownRailroad.com